Lost Atlantis and the Gods of Antiquity
& Plato's History of Atlantis

By Carolus Kiesewetterus
and Manly P. Hall

Copyright © 2019 Lamp of Trismegistus. All rights reserved. No part of this publication may be reproduced or transmitted in any form or by any means, electronic or mechanical, including photocopying, recording, or by any information storage and retrieval system, without permission in writing from Lamp of Trismegistus. Reviewers may quote brief passages.

ISBN: 978-1-63118-431-4

Esoteric Classics

Other Books in this Series and Related Titles

Magical Essays and Instructions by Florence Farr (978-1-63118-418-5)

Ancient Mysteries and Secret Societies by Manly P. Hall (978-1-63118-410-9)

The First and Second Gospels of the Infancy of Jesus Christ by Thomas and James (978-1-63118-415-4)

Ancient Egyptian Mysteries and Hieroglyphics, Modern Freemasonry & Initiation of the Pyramid by various authors (978-1-63118-430-7)

Essays on the Esoteric Tradition of Karma by William Q. Judge, Helena P. Blavatsky and Annie Besant (978-1-63118-426-0)

The Book of the Watchers by Enoch (978-1-63118-416-1)

The Smoky God or A Voyage to the Inner World by Willis George Emerson (978-1-63118-423-9)

Rosa Alchemica, The Tables of Law & The Adoration of the Magi by William Butler Yeats (978-1-63118-421-5)

A Collection of Fiction and Essays by Occult Writers on Supernatural, Metaphysical and Esoteric Subjects by various authors (978-1-63118-712-4)

Occult Symbolism of Animals, Insects, Reptiles, Fish and Birds by Manly P. Hall (978-1-63118-420-8)

The Feminine Occult by various authors (978-1-63118-711-7)

Thirty-One Hymns to the Star Goddess by Frater Achad (978-1-63118-422-2)

Audio Versions are also Available on Audible and iTunes

Table of Contents

Introduction...7

The Lost Atlantis
by Carolus Kiesewetterus...9

-oOo-

Atlantis and the Gods of Antiquity
by Manly P. Hall
Part I...25

Part II: The Myth of the Dying God...36

-oOo-

Plato's History of Atlantis...47

Introduction

The word "esoteric" can be difficult to define. Esotericism in general can be seen less as a system of beliefs and more as a category, which encompasses numerous, different systems of beliefs. It's a bit of juxtaposition, since the word "esoteric" indicates something that few people know about, while the term itself broadly covers numerous philosophies, practices, areas of study and belief systems.

In a greater sense, Esotericism acts as a storehouse for secret knowledge, which is often considered ancient (by *tradition, if not by fact),* passed down from generation to generation, in private. At various times in history, simply possessing the knowledge of some of these subjects, was considered illegal and a jailable offence, if discovered. This usually included such general topics as Alchemy, Qabalah, Hermeticism, Occultism, Ceremonial Magic, Astrology, Divination, Rosicrucianism and so on. Collectively, these areas of study were often referred to as the esoteric sciences.

Sometimes, the outer garment of a subject isn't esoteric, while what is hidden beneath it, is. As an example, Freemasonry isn't necessarily esoteric by nature (at *least not anymore),* but certain signs, passwords and handshakes given to the candidate during their initiation, are in fact, esoteric, in the sense that they are hidden from the general public.

Today, in the twenty-first century, such topics are readily available at bookstores across the country, and numerous mainsteam publishers offer beginners guides and coffee-table volumes on many of these subjects, intended for mass appeal. Books like *"The Secret"* have turned previously arcane topics into household knowledge. All that being the case, however, it isn't to say that there still aren't buried secrets to uncover, ancient wisdom being ignored and forgotten mysteries to be explored. In fact, it is often that we are only able to further our own studies by standing on the shoulders of these disappearing giants.

Lamp of Trismegistus is doing its part to help preserve humanity's esoteric history by making some of these classics available to those students who are seeking to unearth the knowledge of these ancient colossi.

So, be sure to check other titles from our *Esoteric Classics* series, as well as our *Occult Fiction*, *Theosophical Classics*, *Foundations of Freemasonry* and our *Christian Apocrypha Series*. You can also download the audio versions of most of these titles from iTunes or Audible.

The Lost Atlantis

By Carolus Kiesewetterus

An eminent archaeologist lately said that the finding of numerous cases in which ancient traditions have been proved to be true is rapidly altering our attitude towards their authors, and that we are now recovering from a positive mania of incredulity. Archaeological discovery, in fact, is demonstrating what common sense always considered probable - that on the whole the ancient historians were trustworthy as to the main facts of events that happened far nearer to their own time than ours. Much the same thing is taking place in science; recent researches are vindicating many obscure phenomena which materialistic bias had rejected and called superstitious. One of the formerly disdained traditions of antiquity is that a great continent once existed in the Atlantic Ocean, inhabited by civilized man. The truth of this is a matter of peculiar interest to students of Theosophy, for such a civilization, preceding the Stone Ages in Europe, is a necessary factor in the great scheme of world-evolution outlined in the records brought to the attention of the world through the devotion and self-sacrifice of H. P. Blavatsky, the pioneer of Theosophy. Until these clues were brought forward, no student of ancient lore, however learned, could have harmonized the apparently disjointed fragments and allegories of the ancient races.

Far back as we can go we find legends of vanished countries, once inhabited by cultured peoples, and finally overwhelmed by the elements. The story of Noah's Deluge is, of course, the most familiar one to us, but there are many variations, the best known being the Chaldean account, which created such a sensation when it was translated about forty years ago. Within the last few months a far older version has been found in tablets brought from Nippur in Mesopotamia to the University of Pennsylvania. This one is at least four thousand years old, and it is claimed by scholars to be more than a thousand years older than the Biblical account. It gives many details corroborating H. P. Blavatsky's teachings, and in one remarkable passage it gives the names of several of the Antediluvian cities, two of which it states were not drowned in the Flood! China has a similar story of the submersion of the primeval land in consequence of the wickedness of its inhabitants, and the escape of Peiru-un, the Chinese Noah, with his family. India has, of course many traditions of the same event in her sacred books; the followers of Zoroaster have also a few. In the West we find the legend, with variations, in the Scandinavian writings, in Ireland, in Britain, in the traditions of the Seven Cities of Portuguese romance, and, above all, in Greece, where Homer makes several references to the Atlanteans and the island of Ogygia, and where Plato gives a circumstantial account of part of Atlantis which he says he derived through Solon, from the priests of Sais in Egypt. It would take more time than we can spare merely to recite the names of the *sixty-four* separate legends of the kind, which an industrious German scholar, Schwartz, has collected. H. P. Blavatsky says in *The Secret Doctrine*:

> *Had not Diocletian burned the esoteric works of the Egyptians in A. D. 296, together with their books on Alchemy; Caesar*

700,000 rolls at Alexandria; Leo Isaurus 300,000 at Constantinople (eighth cent.) and the Mohammedans all they could lay their sacrilegious hands on -the world might know today more of Atlantis than it does.

The name Atlantis comes from Plato's account, and it is highly significant that, while the words Atlantis and Atlas have no satisfactory etymology in Greek or other European languages, there are numerous similar words in the Mexican Aztec language. A city named Atlan existed near Panama when the Spaniards reached this continent. The Aztecs had colonies as far as Venezuela.

The possible existence of a former continent in the Atlantic Ocean has attracted much attention since H. P. Blavatsky spoke of it, and the great body of scientific opinion, then generally adverse, has so largely changed that her students have the satisfaction today of seeing yet one more of her teachings regarded as more than probable in orthodox scientific quarters.

We are living in an age of quick changes of thought. The time is not far removed when the traditions of the Minoan civilization of Crete - now acknowledged to be of great importance - and the very existence of Pompeii and Troy were looked upon as baseless; when nothing was known of the magnificent monumental structures of Ceylon, of Cambodia, or of Central America and Peru. Comparatively speaking, it is only yesterday that the Egyptian hieroglyphics and the Babylonian cuneiform inscriptions were deciphered; and even today the records of the great Hittite empire cannot be read.

What do we really know of the Etruscans? It is hardly likely, therefore, that much detailed information of submerged civilizations that flourished ages before the earliest of the known empires, and whose remnants perished not less than 9000 years B. C., would be easily accessible to us, particularly when we consider that owing to the incredulity of investigators no systematic search has been made for it. It is a marvel that there is anything to work from. But today, in addition to the clues to the meaning of certain remains and to the references in the old manuscripts given by H. P. Blavatsky, another door has opened to us in the recent researches of science. Geology, oceanography, biology, anthropology, linguistics, and archaeology are all providing us with arguments in its favor. The new facts are so conclusive in regard to a former land connection between America and Africa that geologists are confidently building theories on that hypothesis. Opinion is not quite so unanimous respecting a continental area in the North Atlantic, but even the most skeptical authorities agree that there were once large islands or a great extension of Europe to the westward where there is nothing now but a waste of waters.

In response to a preliminary announcement, widely disseminated in America and Europe and of which we are awaiting further particulars, of the claim that Dr. Paul Schliemann, son of the discoverer of Troy, holds his father's position and undeniable proofs of Atlantean civilization in tangible form, a number of the most eminent scientists, geologists and others, including the names of Sir Norman Lockyer, Professors Hull, and Scharf, have lately written and published their opinions in favor of an Atlantic continent having existed in the Tertiary period. Dr. Hull, F. R. S., President of the Royal Geographical Society of Ireland, etc. has traced the continuation of many of the European river-beds far out under the ocean, and has made a critical examination of the submarine gorges through which they descend, and of the great submarine mountain ranges, some of whose summits appear above water in the shape of islands. He perfectly agrees with the other geologists who point out that these inequalities could never have been formed under water, but must have been carved by agencies acting above sea-level. Dr. Scharf, Director of the Natural History Museum, Dublin, holds that the distribution of plants and animals along the borders of Europe and America can only be explained on the hypothesis of a central continent from which their ancestors radiated. Among a number of similar examples he mentions one of a snail, *Helix hortensis*, which is now found commonly along both shores of the Atlantic and which could never have traveled by water. The study of the present-day animal life in the islands of the Atlantic, and of the fossil remains of the past in the strata of Europe and America has convinced many other scientists of distinction, English, French, and German, such as Edward Suess, Marcel Bertrand, and Louis Germain. M. Pierre Termier, Member of the French Academy of Sciences and Director of the Geological Survey of France, lately pointed out in a lecture on the North Atlantic Ocean (*in which he definitely admitted an Atlantean continent*) that grappling irons had brought up lava from a depth of 10,200 feet in a vitreous condition, that is to say, in a condition which can only be formed under the ordinary atmospheric pressure, and could not have been formed under water. This lava was found far out in the Atlantic, five hundred miles north of the Azores.

All this, and far more than can be even mentioned in the briefest way, proves that Theosophical students cannot be regarded as fanciful in taking seriously the story of a former Atlantic continent. The question of its human habitation, however, is a deeper and more difficult one, but we have, fortunately, no longer to meet the objection that man was not created 11,000 years ago. It is not long since it was dangerous to claim that mankind may have been on earth more than 6000 years. It was dogmatically asserted that the whole Christian scheme of salvation would be upset if it could be proved that man was living twenty or thirty thousand years ago. We were assured that the extremely recent appearance of Jesus could not be explained on the basis of such a vast gulf of time between him and the first man, and so forth. But the orthodoxy of the early nineteenth century is not the orthodoxy of today, and the irresistible pressure of discovery has brushed such arguments aside. We are now discussing whether certain human skulls are - not five or six *thousand years* old, but five or six thousand *centuries* old, or more! and the mystery of the recent appearance of Jesus is beginning to be explained on a broader view of the possibilities of divine justice. The divine Christos Spirit has always been present, even from the beginning of the world, and humanity had not to wait till the birth of Jesus for the first in carnation of that Spirit in human form. As the acknowledged great antiquity of man destroys at one blow the effete arguments, we have, therefore, now only to look for what scraps of evidence we may hope to find testifying to man's presence in Atlantis. It is remarkable that there should be any remaining when we consider the action of Nature's Destructive forces during long periods of time, and the barbarism of man that has destroyed nearly every record of even moderate antiquity. A distressing outrage that has just occurred in Honduras is an example of the risks that even solid stone monuments run. One of the priceless treasures of prehistoric American civilization, a wonderfully carved obelisk or stela of great size at Copan, has been barbarously chopped to pieces and burnt for lime, notwithstanding the supposed protection of the National government. The French government has just barely succeeded in saving from destruction the great aqueduct at Nimes, one of the finest examples of ancient Roman engineering and art. It is to be feared we are not altogether free from the same spirit of vandalism in this country, though a distinct improvement is taking place.

Still, notwithstanding the assaults of Nature and man, there are a few tangible remains that point straight in the direction of the lost Atlantean civilization. We have seen that science requires the existence of the continent to explain the numerous coincidences in regard to modern and ancient forms of life on the two opposite coasts, coincidences, which are far too many and too exact to be the result of chance. Precisely the same demand is made by us from the archaeological point of view. We find certain forms of design in art, certain traditions among the aboriginal peoples, on both continents, which call for a common origin. How can the extraordinary resemblance between the Egyptian pyramids and those of Mexico be explained on the basis of chance? especially when we find such characteristic Egyptian forms as the Sacred Tau, the pre-Christian Cross, the Winged Globe, the Serpent of Wisdom, the Cynocephalus, and others reproduced in American monuments of unknown age. A very curious pyramid, closely resembling the Stepped pyramid at Sakkara in Egypt, is now being explored, in Peru. It is supposed to be a mausoleum of enormous antiquity. The leopard skin, used to clothe certain of the officials in the Eleusinian Greek as well as the Egyptian Mysteries, is duplicated in the carvings of the sacrifices before the altars in Central American temples. The cross, with a dove or some other bird at the top, the symbol of Spirit overshadowing Matter, a widely distributed world-symbol, is found in Central America, There is also striking architectural resemblances between the buildings of Oriental lands and some of the American ones, even in certain details of interest to Masons, but we cannot linger here even to mention them. Though we have, unfortunately, no monuments in this country or Canada of such interest or beauty as those in the South, we have some structures of great significance in our present inquiry. One of these is the Great Serpent Mound, Adams County, Ohio, an immense effigy more than thousand feet long representing a snake swallowing an egg; another is the Serpent Mound in Warren County, Ohio, which is a little larger than the former but minus a head, owing to the encroachment of a stream. Both of these are in commanding positions and well placed for any ceremonies conducted upon or around them to be seen. They would not attract our special attention if they were the only specimens of their kind, but when we find the serpent-and-egg symbol - which represents the ever-advancing Cycles of Time periodically swallowing the manifested universe- widely distributed throughout the ancient world, and that on the opposite side of the Atlantic, in Argyllshire, Scotland, there is precisely such another Serpent Mound, though smaller, their presence here becomes a strong link in our argument.

When we consider the resemblance - even the identity in some cases - of many of the historical, philosophical, and religious legends, and of some of the customs of many of the peoples living on either side of the Atlantic, in connection with the other evidences, the conclusion that there was a common origin is strengthened. Not only do we find in America allegories of the Creation of the World, and of Man, and the Flood story with the destruction of the wicked, in various forms, but all show a likeness to the Oriental allegories. As in ancient Europe and Egypt and in ancient and modern Asia, the belief in the immortality of the soul through reincarnation was widely spread in America. In some districts the native traditions so closely resembled the Bible stories that the Spaniards were at a loss to find a reasonable explanation and fell back upon very quaint theories, it being even suggested that Christian saints must have reached America before Columbus! Theosophy clears up this difficulty. It teaches the Brotherhood of religions, not their antagonism. It shows that the striking likeness between the fundamentals of so many religions in different parts of the globe is due to their common archaic origin, to the time when the illuminated sages taught openly and when religion and science were united. In *Isis Unveiled* H. P. Blavatsky says:

> *There never was nor can there be more than one universal religion, for there can be but one truth concerning God. Like an immense chain whose upper end, the Alpha, remains invisibly emanating from a Deity* - in statu abscondito *in every primitive theology - it encircles our globe in every direction; it leaves not the darkest corner unvisited, before the other end, the Omega, turns back on its way to be again received where it first emanated. On this divine chain was strung the exoteric symbology of every people. . . . Thus it is that all the religious movements of old, in whatever land or under whatever climate, are the expression of the same identical thought, the key to which is the esoteric doctrine.*

And in *The Secret Doctrine* she says:

> *The Secret Doctrine was the universally diffused religion of the ancient and prehistoric world. Proofs of its diffusion, authentic records of its history, a complete chain of documents, showing its character and presence in every land, together with the teaching of all its great Adepts, exist today in the secret crypts of libraries belonging to the Occult Fraternity . . . . all these exist, safe from . . . spoliating hands, to reappear in some more enlightened age.*

While this paper was being prepared two highly significant items of news were received. One tells of the sensational and unexpected discovery of implements and other relics of Tertiary man in Argentina; and the other is the preliminary announcement of the contents of the Navajo Indian archives, nearly two thousand years old, which have just been sent to Pennsylvania University. The report says "these records upset all the theories of the experts who have spent lifetimes in the study of Indian history, and contain facts startling in their revelations and of tremendous importance to ethnologists." It will take several years to analyze thoroughly the records, but it is announced that enough has been deciphered to discredit the theory that the Indians came to America by way of Behring's Straits, an unnecessary one in view of the former existence of Atlantis.

It is the belief of at least one of the most learned students of American languages that unless the Atlantean origin be accepted there is no possibility of a reasonable explanation of their peculiarities.

Though it would be interesting to examine more closely the various lines of evidence briefly sketched, we must pass on to a short consideration of the Atlantis legend in its general relation to Theosophy. And here it is proper to speak of the way a student should proceed who desires to follow up the subject. H. P. Blavatsky gave a broad outline which she had received from her teachers, under the expectation that those who were interested would use it as a sketch whose details might be filled in by new scientific discoveries along the lines we have been considering. This is a rational method for us, and it has proved highly interesting and profitable. Attempts such as we occasionally hear of on the part of indiscreet amateurs in so called occultism, of persons who do not seem to recognize the un-wisdom of their course, to investigate the astral pictures on the psychic planes with their delusions and dangers, are not in harmony with good sense.

One of the fundamentals of Theosophy is that natural processes take place according to periodic laws; in larger or smaller cycles of time. These laws cover the growth and decay of a solar system as well as the life of a butterfly. Science, and even ordinary observation provide us with many examples. In astronomy, for instance, new periodic laws are constantly being discovered. In ordinary life the alternations of sleep and waking and other physiological phenomena are so common that most people take them without a thought of the hidden causes. Physiologists assure us that the mystery of sleep is not fathomed; it is not merely the result of fatigue in the body. The influence of the moon's changes acting on the mind and the body is perfectly well recognized by many physiologists who generally avoid the subject however, apparently for fear of being thought superstitious. Oriental philosophy has studied the subject of cyclic processes in man far more deeply than Western. It is of profound importance and interest.

Among the cyclic periods there are some which are difficult to recognize owing to their length; the larger history of mankind be longs to these. From the wider view of Theosophy the smaller periods of human history are seen as a succession of rises and falls, in which nation after nation climbs its hill of attainment, stays for a while on the heights, and then descends the inevitable path to the next valley. But not empty-handed; in each case something has been learned and impressed upon the deeper consciousness of the component egos. The human soul learns, as a rule, very slowly; it needs long experience of different conditions of earth-life to become fully conscious of its powers. During the progress of its evolution the smaller national cycles are included or covered by the greater racial periods of evolution. One of these was that of Atlantis, and during our life there we gained experience which no other conditions could provide, and which is locked up within. Under unusual circumstances a flash of this latent knowledge is evoked. Call it ancestral memory if you will, or intuition, this knowledge can only be logically explained by the fact that something within us has lived before. Without reincarnation the Evolution principle is incomplete and practically meaningless. Another problem is unsolvable without reincarnation, i. e., the problem of Divine Justice, which faces every religious man when he thinks of the multitudes of unfortunate children who are born into the world with hereditary diseases or handicapped in other ways.

From the scattered legends that have come down to us, the Atlanteans must have attained a high development in arts and sciences. In some of their astronomical records, preserved in the Surya- Siddhanta and other Hindu sacred writings, we find calculations of planetary movements given with such extreme accuracy as must have required long ages of careful observation to attain, and which have deeply impressed every modern astronomer who has studied them. In Egypt traces of ancient observations are found in the zodiac of Denderah, which indicates the position the constellations occupied long before what we know as ancient Egypt existed. The Atlanteans are recorded in the Indian books to have made many scientific inventions of an advanced type, even including flying-machines of a dependable kind. They were also more skillful than we in the art of war, if we may trust the stories of their terrible weapons of destruction. Towards the close of the Atlantean period that decline of virtue took place of which we read in so many ancient legends, and which is said to have angered the gods. Strife arose between the good and the evildoers, until at last Nature took a hand, so to speak, and mankind was preserved from utter degradation by the reconstruction caused by the breaking up of large portions of the continent, and its ultimate disappearance beneath the waters. The last islands vanished about B. C. 9000, as Plato relates. Long before this, refugees had fled to the lands of our cycle, which were assuming something of their present conditions in the later Tertiary period. While a nucleus of civilization was preserved under great difficulties in Central Asia, the larger part of the newly-formed continents was inhabited by very primitive races who had lost most of the wisdom of their remote Atlantean or Lemurian ancestors, and who had to struggle for life against the ferocious animals and the rigors of the Glacial periods. We are now finding a few relics of these low types in the caves and gravel-beds of Western Europe. Some of them are so ape-like in certain features, such as the jaw, and yet have such large and human brains, that biologists are puzzled how to place them. H. P. Blavatsky says that the long period of savagery that we call the Stone Ages was due to the heavy karma of the evildoers of the later Atlantis, who were unable to progress until they had reaped the harvest of their former wrongdoing. Modern civilization, which properly came in with the Aryan race, had a hard battle to reach even its present imperfect state.

In connection with the assertion that Stone Age man was not really primitive man on the upward way, but a decadent, which may seem a very remarkable and revolutionary one, it is worthy of note that while no leader in science will deny the *possibility* of an extremely remote civilization in Atlantis, and while many think it not improbable, at least one, Professor F. Soddy, F. R. S., lecturer in chemistry at Glasgow University and a high authority on radio-activity, in speaking of the enormous power locked up in radium, seriously offers the suggestion that the world may have been plunged into barbarism at some remote age by the misuse of the terrific power of radio activity. Speaking of the possibility of a similar fate happening to us, if we learn how to release that titanic force and are not able to properly control it, he says:

> *The relative positions of Nature and man as servant and master would become reversed, so that even the whole world might be plunged back again under the undisputed sway of Nature, to begin its toilsome way upward through the ages.*

In a measure something of this kind did happen in Atlantis, but the decline of civilization was not due to chance, for the hour of cyclic change had arrived, and the age of the Aryan race was at hand.

The story of Atlantis brings to our attention the fact that the law of cycles cannot be ignored. The practical importance of this law as well as its theoretical interest is enormous, for if we know something about the cyclic periods in our own lives and in the larger life of humanity we shall be able to reinforce the desirable ones and minimize the bad ones; forewarned is forearmed. An understanding of the periodic laws permits us to see something of the ideal framework of the universe, some little glimpse behind the veil of material illusion that will help us in our efforts to step out into a larger life. We have passed in joy and suffering through many strange life- cycles, and, by analogy, we may expect that the future of mankind as a whole will be governed by the same periodic law; but we need not ignorantly linger on the way, once we have realized our true position. Theosophy teaches that the purified man, the one who has fully realized his own divine nature, needs no further incarnation for his own sake, but, having gained self-knowledge - knowledge of the Christos Spirit within - through life after life of unrelaxed effort to destroy the snake of selfishness, needs only to return to help those who are less advanced. It is said that there are many who have gladly chosen this path of renunciation, for the sake of others - the perfection of Brotherhood. To arouse the slumbering souls of those who are not aware of the beauty of the life of Brotherhood, and to call them to unselfish, practical work for others on the most efficient lines, to purify human life, is the purpose of the Theosophical Movement.

Atlantis and the Gods of Antiquity

By Manly P. Hall

PART I

Atlantis is the subject of a short but important article appearing in the Annual Report of the Board of Regents of The Smithsonian Institution for the year ending June 30th, 1915. The author, M. Pierre Termier, a member of the Academy of Sciences and Director of Service of the Geologic Chart of France, in 1912 delivered a lecture on the Atlantean hypothesis before the Institut Océanographique; it is the translated notes of this remarkable lecture that are published in the Smithsonian report.

"After a long period of disdainful indifference," writes M. Termier, "observe how in the last few years science is returning to the study of Atlantis. How many naturalists, geologists, zoologists, or botanists are asking one another today whether Plato has not transmitted to us, with slight amplification, a page from the actual history of mankind. No affirmation is yet permissible; but it seems more and more evident that a vast region, continental or made up of great islands, has collapsed west of the Pillars of Hercules, otherwise called the Strait of Gibraltar, and that its collapse occurred in the not far distant past. In any event, the question of Atlantis is placed anew before men of science; and since I do not believe that it can ever be solved without the aid of oceanography, I have thought it natural to discuss it here, in this temple of maritime science, and to call to such a problem, long scorned but now being revived, the attention of oceanographers, as well as the attention of those who, though immersed in the tumult of cities, lend an ear to the distant murmur of the sea."

In his lecture M. Termier presents geologic, geographic, and zoologic data in substantiation of the Atlantis theory. Figuratively draining the entire bed of the Atlantic Ocean, he considers the inequalities of its basin and cites locations on a line from the Azores to Iceland where dredging has brought lava to the surface from a depth of 3,000 meters. The volcanic nature of the islands now existing in the Atlantic Ocean corroborates Plato's statement that the Atlantean continent was destroyed by volcanic cataclysms. M. Termier also advances the conclusions of a young French zoologist, M. Louis Germain, who admitted the existence of an Atlantic continent connected with the Iberian Peninsula and with Mauritania and prolonged toward the south so as to include some regions of desert climate. M. Termier concludes his lecture with a graphic picture of the engulfment of that continent.

The description of the Atlantean civilization given by Plato in the *Critias* may be summarized as follows. In the first ages the gods divided the earth among themselves, proportioning it according to their respective dignities. Each became the peculiar deity of his own allotment and established therein temples to himself, ordained a priestcraft, and instituted a system of sacrifice. To Poseidon was given the sea and the island continent of Atlantis. In the midst of the island was a mountain which was the dwelling place of three earth-born primitive human beings--Evenor; his wife, Leucipe; and their only daughter, Cleito. The maiden was very beautiful, and after the sudden death of her parents she was wooed by Poseidon, who begat by her five pairs of male children. Poseidon apportioned his continent among these ten, and Atlas, the eldest, he made overlord of the other nine. Poseidon further called the country *Atlantis* and the surrounding sea the *Atlantic* in honor of Atlas. Before the birth of his ten sons, Poseidon divided the continent and the coastwise sea into concentric zones of land and water, which were as perfect as though turned upon a lathe. Two zones of land and three of water surrounded the central island, which Poseidon caused to be irrigated with two springs of water--one warm and the other cold.

The descendants of Atlas continued as rulers of Atlantis, and with wise government and industry elevated the country to a position of surpassing dignity. The natural resources of Atlantis were apparently limitless. Precious metals were mined, wild animals domesticated, and perfumes distilled from its fragrant flowers. While enjoying the abundance natural to their semitropic location, the Atlanteans employed themselves also in the erection of palaces, temples, and docks. They bridged the zones of sea and later dug a deep canal to connect the outer ocean with the central island, where stood the palaces And temple of Poseidon, which excelled all other structures in magnificence. A network of bridges and canals was created by the Atlanteans to unite the various parts of their kingdom.

Plato then describes the white, black, and red stones which they quarried from beneath their continent and used in the construction of public buildings and docks. They circumscribed each of the land zones with a wall, the outer wall being covered with brass, the middle with tin, and the inner, which encompassed the citadel, with orichalch. The citadel, on the central island, contained the pal aces, temples, and other public buildings. In its center, surrounded by a wall of gold, was a sanctuary dedicated to Cleito and Poseidon. Here the first ten princes of the island were born and here each year their descendants brought offerings. Poseidon's own temple, its exterior entirely covered with silver and its pinnacles with gold, also stood within the citadel. The interior of the temple was of ivory, gold, silver, and orichalch, even to the pillars and floor. The temple contained a colossal statue of Poseidon standing in a chariot drawn by six winged horses, about him a hundred Nereids riding on dolphins. Arranged outside the building were golden statues of the first ten kings and their wives.

In the groves and gardens were hot and cold springs. There were numerous temples to various deities, places of exercise for men and for beasts, public baths, and a great race course for horses. At various vantage points on the zones were fortifications, and to the great harbor came vessels from every maritime nation. The zones were so thickly populated that the sound of human voices was ever in the air.

That part of Atlantis facing the sea was described as lofty and precipitous, but about the central city was a plain sheltered by mountains renowned for their size, number, and beauty. The plain yielded two crops each year,, in the winter being watered by rains and in the summer by immense irrigation canals, which were also used for transportation. The plain was divided into sections, and in time of war each section supplied its quota of fighting men and chariots.

The ten governments differed from each other in details concerning military requirements. Each of the kings of Atlantis had complete control over his own kingdom, but their mutual relationships were governed by a code engraved by the first ten kings on a column of orichalch standing in the temple of Poseidon. At alternate intervals of five and six years a pilgrimage was made to this temple that equal honor might be conferred upon both the odd and the even numbers. Here, with appropriate sacrifice, each king renewed his oath of loyalty upon the sacred inscription. Here also the kings donned azure robes and sat in judgment. At daybreak they wrote their sentences upon a golden tablet: and deposited them with their robes as memorials. The chief laws of the Atlantean kings were that they should not take up arms against each other and that they should come to the assistance of any of their number who was attacked. In matters of war and great moment the final decision was in the hands of the direct descendants of the family of Atlas. No king had the power of life and death over his kinsmen without the assent of a majority of the ten.

Plato concludes his description by declaring that it was this great empire which attacked the Hellenic states. This did not occur, however, until their power and glory had lured the Atlantean kings from the pathway of wisdom and virtue. Filled with false ambition, the rulers of Atlantis determined to conquer the entire world. Zeus, perceiving the wickedness of the Atlanteans, gathered the gods into his holy habitation and addressed them. Here Plato's narrative comes to an abrupt end, for the *Critias* was never finished. In the *Timæus* is a further description of Atlantis, supposedly given to Solon by an Egyptian priest and which concludes as follows:

> "But afterwards there occurred violent earthquakes and floods; and in a single day and night of rain all your warlike men in a body sank into the earth, and the island of Atlantis in like manner disappeared, and was sunk beneath the sea. And that is the reason why the sea in those parts is impassable and impenetrable, because there is such a quantity of shallow mud in the way; and this was caused by the subsidence of the island."

In the introduction to his translation of the *Timæus*, Thomas Taylor quotes from a *History of Ethiopia* written by Marcellus, which contains the following reference to Atlantis: "For they relate that in their time there were seven islands in the Atlantic sea, sacred to Proserpine; and besides these, three others of an immense magnitude; one of which was sacred to Pluto, another to Ammon, and another, which is the middle of these, and is of a thousand stadia, to Neptune." Crantor, commenting upon Plato, asserted that the Egyptian priests declared the story of Atlantis to be written upon pillars which were still preserved circa 300 B.C. Ignatius Donnelly, who gave the subject of Atlantis profound study, believed that horses were first domesticated by the Atlanteans, for which reason they have always been considered peculiarly sacred to Poseidon.

From a careful consideration of Plato's description of Atlantis it is evident that the story should not be regarded as wholly historical but rather as both allegorical and historical. Origen, Porphyry, Proclus, Iamblichus, and Syrianus realized that the story concealed a profound philosophical mystery, but they disagreed as to the actual interpretation. Plato's Atlantis symbolizes the threefold nature of both the universe and the human body. The ten kings of Atlantis are the *tetractys,* or numbers, which are born as five pairs of opposites. The numbers 1 to 10 rule every creature, and the numbers, in turn, are under the control of the Monad, or 1-- the Eldest among them.

With the trident scepter of Poseidon these kings held sway over the inhabitants of the seven small and three great islands comprising Atlantis. Philosophically, the ten islands symbolize the triune powers of the Superior Deity and the seven regents who bow before His eternal throne. If Atlantis be considered as the archetypal sphere, then its immersion signifies the descent of rational, organized consciousness into the illusionary, impermanent realm of irrational, mortal ignorance. Both the sinking of Atlantis and the Biblical story of the "fall of man" signify spiritual involution--a prerequisite to conscious evolution.

Either the initiated Plato used the Atlantis allegory to achieve two widely different ends or else the accounts preserved by the Egyptian priests were tampered with to perpetuate the secret doctrine. This does not mean to imply that Atlantis is purely mythological, but it overcomes the most serious obstacle to acceptance of the Atlantis theory, namely, the fantastic accounts of its origin, size, appearance, and date of destruction--9600 B.C. In the midst of the central island of

Atlantis was a lofty mountain which cast a shadow five thousand stadia in extent and whose summit touched the sphere of *æther*. This is the axle mountain of the world, sacred among many races and symbolic of the human head, which rises out of the four elements of the body. This sacred mountain, upon whose summit stood the temple of the gods, gave rise to the stories of Olympus, Meru, and Asgard. The City of the Golden Gates--the capital of Atlantis--is the one now preserved among numerous religions as the *City of the Gods* or the *Holy City*. Here is the archetype of the New Jerusalem, with its streets paved with gold and its twelve gates shining with precious stones.

"The history of Atlantis," writes Ignatius Donnelly, "is the key of the Greek mythology. There can be no question that these gods of Greece were human beings. The tendency to attach divine attributes to great earthly rulers is one deeply implanted in human nature."

The same author sustains his views by noting that the deities of the Greek pantheon were nor looked upon as creators of the universe but rather as regents set over it by its more ancient original fabricators. The Garden of Eden from which humanity was driven by a flaming sword is perhaps an allusion to the earthly paradise supposedly located west of the Pillars of Hercules and destroyed by volcanic cataclysms. The Deluge legend may be traced also to the Atlantean inundation, during which a "world" was destroyed by water.,

Was the religious, philosophic, and scientific knowledge possessed by the priestcrafts of antiquity secured from Atlantis, whose submergence obliterated every vestige of its part in the drama of world progress? Atlantean sun worship has been perpetuated in the ritualism and ceremonialism of both Christianity and pagandom. Both the cross and the serpent were Atlantean emblems of divine wisdom. The divine (Atlantean) progenitors of the Mayas and Quichés of Central America coexisted within the green and azure radiance of Gucumatz, the "plumed" serpent. The six sky-born sages came into manifestation as centers of light bound together or synthesized by the seventh--and chief--of their order, the "feathered" snake. The title of "winged" or "plumed" snake was applied to Quetzalcoatl, or Kukulcan, the Central American initiate. The center of the Atlantean Wisdom-Religion was presumably a great pyramidal temple standing on the brow of a plateau rising in the midst of the City of the Golden Gates. From here the Initiate-Priests of the Sacred Feather went forth, carrying the keys of Universal Wisdom to the uttermost parts of the earth.

The mythologies of many nations contain accounts of gods who "came out of the sea." Certain *shamans* among the American Indians tell of holy men dressed in birds' feathers and wampum who rose out of the blue waters and instructed them in the arts and crafts. Among the legends of the Chaldeans is that of Oannes, a partly amphibious creature who came out of the sea and taught the savage peoples along the shore to read and write, till the soil, cultivate herbs for healing, study the stars, establish rational forms of government, and become conversant with the sacred Mysteries. Among the Mayas, Quetzalcoatl, the Savior-God (whom some Christian scholars believe to have been St. Thomas), issued from the waters and, after instructing the people in the essentials of civilization, rode out to sea on a magic raft of serpents to escape the wrath of the fierce god of the Fiery Mirror, Tezcatlipoca.

May it not have been that these demigods of a fabulous age who, Esdras-like, came out of the sea were Atlantean priests? All that primitive man remembered of the Atlanteans was the glory of their golden ornaments, the transcendency of their wisdom, and the sanctity of their symbols--the cross and the serpent. That they came in ships was soon forgotten, for untutored minds considered even boats as supernatural. Wherever the Atlanteans proselyted they erected pyramids and temples patterned after the great sanctuary in the City of the Golden Gates. Such is the origin of the pyramids of Egypt, Mexico, and Central America. The mounds in Normandy and Britain, as well as those of the American Indians, are remnants of a similar culture. In the midst of the Atlantean program of world colonization and conversion, the cataclysms which sank Atlantis began. The Initiate-Priests of the Sacred Feather who promised to come back to their missionary settlements never returned; and after the lapse of centuries tradition preserved only a fantastic account of gods who came from a place where the sea now is.

H. P. Blavatsky thus sums up the causes which precipitated the Atlantean disaster: "Under the evil insinuations of their demon, Thevetat, the Atlantis-race became a nation of wicked *magicians*. In consequence of this, war was declared, the story of which would be too long to narrate; its substance may be found in the disfigured allegories of the race of Cain, the giants, and that of Noah and his righteous family. The conflict came to an end by the submersion of the Atlantis; which finds its imitation in the stories of the Babylonian and Mosaic flood: The giants and magicians '…and all flesh died …and every man.' All except Xisuthrus and Noah, who are substantially identical with the great Father of the Thlinkithians in the *Popol Vuh,* or the sacred book of the Guatemaleans, which also tells of his escaping in a large boat, like the Hindu Noah--Vaiswasvata."

From the Atlanteans the world has received not only the heritage of arts and crafts, philosophies and sciences, ethics and religions, but also the heritage of hate, strife, and perversion. The Atlanteans instigated the first war; and it has been said that all subsequent wars were fought in a fruitless effort to justify the first one and right the wrong which it caused. Before Atlantis sank, its spiritually illumined Initiates, who realized that their land was doomed because it had departed from the Path of Light, withdrew from the ill-fated continent. Carrying with them the sacred and secret doctrine, these Atlanteans established themselves in Egypt, where they became its first "divine" rulers. Nearly all the great cosmologic myths forming the foundation of the various sacred books of the world are based upon the Atlantean Mystery rituals.

PART II

The Myth of the Dying God

The myth of *Tammuz* and *Ishtar* is one of the earliest examples of the dying-god allegory, probably antedating 4000 B. C. The imperfect condition of the tablets upon which the legends are inscribed makes it impossible to secure more than a fragmentary account of the Tammuz rites. Being the esoteric god of the sun, Tammuz did not occupy a position among the first deities venerated by the Babylonians, who for lack of deeper knowledge looked upon him as a god of agriculture or a vegetation spirit. Originally he was described as being one of the guardians of the gates of the underworld. Like many other Savior-Gods, he is referred to as a "shepherd" or "the lord of the shepherd seat." Tammuz occupies the remarkable position of son and husband of Ishtar, the Babylonian and Assyrian Mother-goddess. Ishtar--to whom the planer Venus was sacred--was the most widely venerated deity of the Babylonian and Assyrian pantheon. She was probably identical with Ashterorh, Astarte, and Aphrodite. The story of her descent into the underworld in search presumably for the sacred elixir which alone could restore Tammuz to life is the key to the ritual of her Mysteries. Tammuz, whose annual festival took place just before the summer solstice, died in midsummer in the ancient month which bore his name, and was mourned with elaborate ceremonies. The manner of his death is unknown, but some of the accusations made against Ishtar by Izdubar

(Nimrod) would indicate that she, indirectly at least, had contributed to his demise. The resurrection of Tammuz was the occasion of great rejoicing, at which time he was hailed as a "redeemer" of his people.

With outspread wings, Ishtar, the daughter of Sin (the Moon), sweeps downward to the gates of death. The house of darkness--the dwelling of the god Irkalla--is described as "the place of no return." It is without light; the nourishment of those who dwell therein is dust and their food is mud. Over the bolts on the door of the house of Irkalla is scattered dust, and the keepers of the house are covered with feathers like birds. Ishtar demands that the keepers open the gates, declaring that if they do not she will shatter the doorposts and strike the hinges and raise up dead devourers of the living. The guardians of the gates beg her to be patient while they go to the queen of Hades from whom they secure permission to admit Ishtar, but only in the same manner as all others came to this dreary house. Ishtar thereupon descends through the seven gates which lead downward into the depths of the underworld. At the first gate the great crown is removed from her head, at the second gate the earrings from her ears, at the third gate the necklace from her neck, at the fourth gate the ornaments from her breast, at the fifth gate the girdle from her waist, at the sixth gate the bracelets from her hands and feet, and at the seventh gate the covering cloak of her body. Ishtar remonstrates as each successive article of apparel is taken from her, bur the guardian tells her that this is the experience of all who enter the somber domain of death. Enraged upon beholding Ishtar, the Mistress of Hades inflicts upon her all manner of disease and imprisons her in the underworld.

As Ishtar represents the spirit of fertility, her loss prevents the ripening of the crops and the maturing of all life upon the earth.

In this respect the story parallels the legend of Persephone. The gods, realizing that the loss of Ishtar is disorganizing all Nature, send a messenger to the underworld and demand her release. The Mistress of Hades is forced to comply, and the water of life is poured over Ishtar. Thus cured of the infirmities inflicted on her, she retraces her way upward through the seven gates, at each of which she is reinvested with the article of apparel which the guardians had removed. No record exists that Ishtar secured the water of life which would have wrought the resurrection of Tammuz.

The myth of Ishtar symbolizes the descent of the human spirit through the seven worlds, or spheres of the sacred planets, until finally, deprived of its spiritual adornments, it incarnates in the physical body-- Hades--where the mistress of that body heaps every form of sorrow and misery upon the imprisoned consciousness. The waters of life--the secret doctrine--cure the diseases of ignorance; and the spirit, ascending again to its divine source, regains its God-given adornments as it passes upward through the rings of the planets.

Another Mystery ritual among the Babylonians and Assyrians was that of Merodach and the Dragon. Merodach, the creator of the inferior universe, slays a horrible monster and out of her body forms the universe. Here is the probable source of the so-called Christian allegory of St. George and the Dragon.

The Mysteries of *Adonis,* or *Adoni,* were celebrated annually in many parts of Egypt, Phœnicia, and Biblos. The name *Adonis,* or *Adoni,* means "Lord" and was a designation applied to the sun and later borrowed by the Jews as the exoteric name of their God. Smyrna, mother of Adonis, was turned into a tree by the gods and after a time the bark burst open and the infant Savior issued forth. According to one account, he was liberated by a wild boar which split the wood of the maternal tree with its tusks. Adonis was born at midnight of the 24th of December, and through his unhappy death a Mystery rite was established that wrought the salvation of his people. In the Jewish month of Tammuz (another name for this deity) he was gored to death by a wild boar sent by the god Ars (Mars). The *Adoniasmos* was the ceremony of lamenting the premature death of the murdered god.

In Ezekiel viii. 14, it is written that women were weeping for Tammuz (Adonis) at the north gate of the Lord's House in Jerusalem. Sir James George Frazer cites Jerome thus: "He tells us that Bethlehem, the traditionary birthplace of the Lord, was shaded by a grove of that still older Syrian Lord, Adonis, and that where the infant Jesus had wept, the lover of Venus was bewailed." The effigy of a wild boar is said to have been set over one of the gates of Jerusalem in honor of Adonis, and his rites celebrated in the grotto of the Nativity at Bethlehem. Adonis as the "gored" (or "god") man is one of the keys to Sir Francis Bacon's use of the "wild boar" in his cryptic symbolism.

Adonis was originally an androgynous deity who represented the solar power which in the winter was destroyed by the evil principle of cold--the boar. After three days (months) in the tomb, Adonis rose triumphant on the 25th day of March, amidst the acclamation of his priests and followers, "He is risen!" Adonis was born out of a myrrh tree. Myrrh, the symbol of death because of its connection with the process of embalming, was one of the gifts brought by the three Magi to the manger of Jesus.

In the Mysteries of Adonis the neophyte passed through the symbolic death of the god and, "raised" by the priests, entered into the blessed state of redemption made possible by the sufferings of Adonis. Nearly all authors believe Adonis to have been originally a vegetation god directly connected with the growth and maturing of flowers and fruits. In support of this viewpoint they describe the "gardens of Adonis, " which were small baskets of earth in which seeds were planted and nurtured for a period of eight days. When those plants prematurely died for lack of sufficient earth, they were considered emblematic of the murdered Adonis and were usually cast into the sea with images of the god.

In Phrygia there existed a remarkable school of religious philosophy which centered around the life and untimely fate of another Savior-God known as *Atys*, or *Attis*, by many considered synonymous with Adonis. This deity was born at midnight on the 24th day of December. Of his death there are two accounts. In one he was gored to death like Adonis; in the other he emasculated himself under a pine tree and there died. His body was taken to a cave by the Great Mother (Cybele), where it remained through the ages without decaying. To the rites of Atys the modern world is indebted for the symbolism of the Christmas tree. Atys imparted his immortality to the tree beneath which he died, and Cybele took the tree with her when she removed the body. Atys remained three days in the tomb, rose upon a date corresponding with Easter morn, and by this resurrection overcame death for all who were initiated into his Mysteries.

"In the Mysteries of the Phrygians, "says Julius Firmicus, "which are called those of the MOTHER OF THE GODS, every year a PINE TREE is cut down and in the inside of the tree the image of a YOUTH is tied in! In the Mysteries of Isis the trunk of a PINE TREE is cut: the middle of the trunk is nicely hollowed out; the idol of Osiris made from those hollowed pieces is BURIED. In the Mysteries of Proserpine a tree cut is put together into the effigy and form of the VIRGIN, and when it has been carried within the city it is MOURNED 40 nights, but the fortieth night it is BURNED!"

The Mysteries of Atys included a sacramental meal during which the neophyte ate out of a drum and drank from a cymbal. After being baptized by the blood of a bull, the new initiate was fed entirely on milk to symbolize that he was still a philosophical infant, having but recently been born out of the sphere of materiality. Is there a possible connection between this lacteal diet prescribed by the Attic rite and St. Paul's allusion to the food for spiritual babes? Sallust gives a key to the esoteric interpretation of the Attic rituals. Cybele, the Great Mother, signifies the vivifying powers of the universe, and Atys that aspect of the spiritual intellect which is suspended between the divine and animal spheres. The Mother of the gods, loving Atys, gave him a starry hat, signifying celestial powers, but Atys (mankind), falling in love with a nymph (symbolic of the lower animal propensities), forfeited his divinity and lost his creative powers. It is thus evident that Atys represents the human consciousness and that his Mysteries are concerned with the re-attainment of the starry hat.

The rites of *Sabazius* were very similar to those of Bacchus and it is generally believed that the two deities are identical. Bacchus was born at Sabazius, or Sabaoth, and these names are frequently assigned to him. The Sabazian Mysteries were performed at night, and the ritual included the drawing of a live snake across the breast of the candidate. Clement of Alexandria writes: "The token of the Sabazian Mysteries to the initiated is 'the deity gliding over the breast.'" A golden serpent was the symbol of Sabazius because this deity represented the annual renovation of the world by the solar power. The Jews borrowed the name Sabaoth from these Mysteries and adopted it as one of the appellations of their supreme God. During the time the Sabazian Mysteries were celebrated in Rome, the cult gained many votaries and later influenced the symbolism of Christianity.

The Cabiric Mysteries of Samothrace were renowned among the ancients, being next to the Eleusinian in public esteem. Herodotus declares that the Samothracians received their doctrines, especially those concerning Mercury, from the Pelasgians. Little is known concerning the Cabiric rituals, for they were enshrouded in the profoundest secrecy. Some regard the Cabiri as seven in number and refer to them as "the Seven

Spirits of fire before the throne of Saturn." Others believe the Cabiri to be the seven sacred wanderers, later called the planets.

While a vast number of deities are associated with the Samothracian Mysteries, the ritualistic drama centers around four brothers. The first three--Aschieros, Achiochersus, and Achiochersa--attack and murder the fourth--Cashmala (or Cadmillus). Dionysidorus, however, identifies Aschieros with Demeter, Achiochersus with Pluto, Achiochersa with Persephone, and Cashmala with Hermes. Alexander Wilder notes that in the Samothracian ritual "Cadmillus is made to include the Theban Serpent-god, Cadmus, the Thoth of Egypt, the Hermes of the Greeks, and the Emeph or Æsculapius of the Alexandrians and Phœnicians. " Here again is a repetition of the story of Osiris, Bacchus, Adonis, Balder, and Hiram Abiff. The worship of Atys and Cybele was also involved in the Samothracian Mysteries. In the rituals of the Cabiri is to be traced a form of pine-tree worship, for this tree, sacred to Atys, was first trimmed into the form of a cross and then cut down in honor of the murdered god whose body was discovered at its foot.

"If you wish to inspect the orgies of the Corybantes, " writes Clement, "Then know that, having killed their third brother, they covered the head of the dead body with a purple cloth, crowned it, and carrying it on the point of a spear, buried it under the roots of Olympus. These mysteries are, in short, murders and funerals. [*This ante-Nicene Father in his efforts to defame the pagan rites apparently ignores the fact that, like the Cabirian martyr, Jesus Christ was foully betrayed, tortured, and finally murdered!*] And the priests Of these rites, who are called kings of the sacred rites by those whose business it is to name them, give additional strangeness to the tragic occurrence, by forbidding parsley with the roots from being placed on the table, for they think that parsley grew from the Corybantic blood that flowed forth; just as the women, in celebrating the Thesmophoria, abstain from eating the seeds of the pomegranate, which have fallen on the ground, from the idea that pomegranates sprang from the drops of the blood of Dionysus. Those Corybantes also they call Cabiric; and the ceremony itself they announce as the Cabiric mystery."

The Mysteries of the Cabiri were divided into three degrees, the first of which celebrated the death of Cashmala, at the hands of his three brothers; the second, the discovery of his mutilated body, the parts of which had been found and gathered after much labor; and the third--accompanied by great rejoicing and happiness--his resurrection and the consequent salvation of the world. The temple of the Cabiri at Samothrace contained a number of curious divinities, many of them misshapen creatures representing the elemental powers of Nature, possibly the Bacchic Titans. Children were initiated into the Cabirian cult with the same dignity as adults, and criminals who reached the sanctuary were safe from pursuit. The Samothracian rites were particularly concerned with navigation, the Dioscuri--Castor and Pollux, or the gods of navigation--being among those propitiated by members of that cult. The Argonautic expedition, listening to the advice of Orpheus, stopped at the island of Samothrace for the purpose of having its members initiated into the Cabiric rites.

Herodotus relates that when Cambyses entered the

temple of the Cabiri he was unable to restrain his mirth at seeing before him the figure of a man standing upright and, facing the man, the figure of a woman standing on her head. Had Cambyses been acquainted with the principles of divine astronomy, he would have realized that he was then in the presence of the key to universal equilibrium. "'I ask,' says Voltaire, 'who were these Hierophants, these sacred Freemasons, who celebrated their Ancient Mysteries of Samothracia, and whence came they and their gods Cabiri?'" Clement speaks of the Mysteries of the Cabiri as "the sacred Mystery of a brother slain by his brethren," and the "Cabiric death" was one of the secret symbols of antiquity. Thus the allegory of the Self murdered by the not-self is perpetuated through the religious mysticism of all peoples. The *philosophic death* and the *philosophic resurrection* are the Lesser and the Greater Mysteries respectively.

A curious aspect of the *dying-god* myth is that of the Hanged Man. The most important example of this peculiar conception is found in the Odinic rituals where Odin hangs himself for nine nights from the branches of the World Tree and upon the same occasion also pierces his own side with the sacred spear. As the result of this great sacrifice, Odin, while suspended over the depths of Nifl-heim, discovered by meditation the runes or alphabets by which later the records of his people were preserved. Because of this remarkable experience, Odin is sometimes shown seated on a gallows tree and he became the patron deity of all who died by the noose. Esoterically, the Hanged Man is the human spirit which is suspended from heaven by a single thread. Wisdom, not death, is the reward for this voluntary sacrifice during which the human soul, suspended above the world of illusion, and meditating upon its unreality, is rewarded by the achievement of self-realization.

From a consideration of all these ancient and secret rituals it becomes evident that the mystery of the *dying god* was universal among the illumined and venerated colleges of the sacred teaching. This mystery has been perpetuated in Christianity in the crucifixion and death of the God-man-Jesus the Christ. The secret import of this world tragedy and the Universal Martyr must be rediscovered if Christianity is to reach the heights attained by the pagans in the days of their philosophic supremacy. The myth of the dying god is the key to both universal and individual redemption and regeneration, and those who do not comprehend the true nature of this supreme allegory are not privileged to consider themselves either wise or truly religious.

Plato's History of Atlantis

Plato has preserved for us the history of Atlantis. If our views are correct, it is one of the most valuable records which have come down to us from antiquity.

Plato lived 400 years before the birth of Christ. His ancestor, Solon, was the great law-giver of Athens 600 years before the Christian era. Solon visited Egypt. Plutarch says, "Solon attempted in verse a large description, or rather fabulous account of the Atlantic Island, which he had learned from the wise men of Sais, and which particularly concerned the Athenians; but by reason of his age, not want of leisure (as Plato would have it), he was apprehensive the work would be too much for him, and therefore did not go through with it. These verses are a proof that business was not the hinderance:

"'I grow in learning as I grow in age.'

And again:

"'Wine, wit, and beauty still their charms bestow,
Light all the shades of life, and cheer us as we go.'

"Plato, ambitious to cultivate and adorn the subject of the Atlantic Island, as a delightful spot in some fair field unoccupied, to which also be had some claim by reason of his being related to Solon, laid out magnificent courts and enclosures, and erected a grand entrance to it, such as no other story, fable, or Poem ever had. But, as he began it late, he ended his life before the work, so that the more the reader is delighted with the part that is written, the more regret he has to find it unfinished."

There can be no question that Solon visited Egypt. The causes of his departure from Athens, for a period of ten years, are fully explained by Plutarch. He dwelt, be tells us,

"On the Canopian shore, by Nile's deep mouth."

There be conversed upon points of philosophy and history with the most learned of the Egyptian priests. He was a man of extraordinary force and penetration of mind, as his laws and his sayings, which have been preserved to us, testify. There is no improbability in the statement that be commenced in verse a history and description of Atlantis, which be left unfinished at his death; and it requires no great stretch of the imagination to believe that this manuscript reached the hands of his successor and descendant, Plato; a scholar, thinker, and historian like himself, and, like himself, one of the profoundest minds of the ancient world. the Egyptian priest had said to Solon, "You have no antiquity of history, and no history of antiquity;" and Solon doubtless realized fully the vast importance of a record which carried human history back, not only thousands of years before the era of Greek civilization, but many thousands of years before even the establishment of the kingdom of Egypt; and be was anxious to preserve for his half-civilized countrymen this inestimable record of the past.

We know of no better way to commence a book about Atlantis than by giving in full the record preserved by Plato. It is as follows:

Critias. Then listen, Socrates, to a strange tale, which is, however, certainly true, as Solon, who was the wisest of the seven sages, declared. He was a relative and great friend of my great-grandfather, Dropidas, as be himself says in several of his poems; and Dropidas told Critias, my grandfather, who remembered, and told us, that there were of old great and marvelous actions of the Athenians, which have passed into oblivion through time and the destruction of the human race and one in particular, which was the greatest of them all, the recital of which will be a suitable testimony of our gratitude to you....

Socrates. Very good; and what is. this ancient famous action of which Critias spoke, not as a mere legend, but as a veritable action of the Athenian State, which Solon recounted!

Critias. I will tell an old-world story which I heard from an aged man; for Critias was, as be said, at that time nearly ninety years of age, and I was about ten years of age. Now the day was that day of the Apaturia which is called the registration of youth; at which, according to custom, our parents gave prizes for recitations, and the poems of several poets were recited by us boys, and many of us sung the poems of Solon, which were new at the time. One of our tribe, either because this was his real opinion, or because he thought that he would please Critias, said that, in his judgment, Solon was not only the wisest of men but the noblest of poets. The old man, I well remember, brightened up at this, and said, smiling: "Yes, Amynander, if Solon had only, like other poets, made poetry the business of his life, and had completed the tale which he brought with him from Egypt, and had not been compelled, by reason of the factions and troubles which he found stirring in this country when he came home, to attend to other matters, in my opinion be would have been as famous as Homer, or Hesiod, or any poet."

"And what was that poem about, Critias?" said the person who addressed him.

"About the greatest action which the Athenians ever did, and which ought to have been most famous, but which, through the lapse of time and the destruction of the actors, has not come down to us."

"Tell us," said the other, "the whole story, and how and from whom Solon heard this veritable tradition."

He replied: "At the head of the Egyptian Delta, where the river Nile divides, there is a certain district which is called the district of Sais, and the great city of the district is also called Sais, and is the city from which Amasis the king was sprung. And the citizens have a deity who is their foundress: she is called in the Egyptian tongue Neith, which is asserted by them to be the same whom the Hellenes called Athene. Now, the citizens of this city are great lovers of the Athenians, and say that they are in some way related to them. Thither came Solon, who was received by them with great honor; and be asked the priests, who were most skillful in such matters, about antiquity, and made the discovery that neither he nor any other Hellene knew anything worth mentioning about the times of old. On one occasion, when he was drawing them on to speak of antiquity, he began to tell about the most ancient things in our part of the world--about Phoroneus, who is called 'the first,' and about Niobe; and, after the Deluge, to tell of the lives of Deucalion and Pyrrha; and he traced the genealogy of their descendants, and attempted to reckon bow many years old were the events of which he was speaking, and to give the dates. Thereupon, one of the priests, who was of very great age; said, 'O Solon, Solon, you Hellenes are but children, and there is never an old man who is an Hellene.' Solon, bearing this, said, 'What do you mean?' 'I mean to say,' he replied, 'that in mind you are all young; there is no old opinion handed down among you by ancient tradition, nor any science which is hoary with age. And I will tell you the reason of this: there have been, and there will be again, many destructions of mankind arising out of many causes. There is a story which even you have preserved, that once upon a time Phaëthon, the son of Helios, having yoked the steeds in his father's chariot, because he was not able to drive them in the path of his father, burnt up all that was upon the earth, and was himself destroyed by a thunderbolt. Now, this has the form of a myth, but really signifies a declination of the bodies moving around the earth and in the heavens, and a great conflagration of things upon the earth recurring at long intervals of time: when this happens, those who live upon the mountains and in dry and lofty places are more liable to destruction than those who dwell by rivers or on the sea-shore; and from this calamity the Nile, who is our never-failing savior, saves and delivers us. When, on the other hand, the gods purge the earth with a deluge of water, among you herdsmen and shepherds on the mountains are the survivors, whereas those of you who live in cities are carried by the rivers into the sea; but in this country neither at that time nor at any other does the water come from above on the fields, having always a tendency to come up from below, for which reason the things preserved here are said to be the oldest. The fact is, that wherever the extremity of winter frost or of summer sun does not prevent, the human race is always increasing at times, and at other times diminishing in numbers. And whatever happened either in your country or in ours, or in any other region of which we are informed--if any action which is noble or great, or in any other way remarkable has taken place, all that has been written down of old, and is preserved in our temples; whereas you and other nations are just being provided with letters and the other things which States require; and then, at the usual period, the stream from heaven descends like a pestilence, and leaves only those of you who are destitute of letters and education; and thus you have to begin all over again as children, and know nothing of what happened in ancient times, either among us or among yourselves. As for those genealogies of yours which you have recounted to us, Solon, they are no better than the tales of children; for, in the first place, you remember one deluge only, whereas there were many of them; and, in the next place, you do not know that there dwelt in your land the fairest and noblest race of men which ever lived, of whom you and your whole city are but a seed or remnant. And this was unknown to you, because for many generations the survivors of that destruction died and made no sign. For there was a time, Solon, before that great deluge of all, when the city which now is Athens was first in war, and was preeminent for the excellence of her laws, and is said to have performed the noblest deeds, and to have had the fairest constitution of any of which tradition tells, under the face of heaven.' Solon marveled at this, and earnestly requested the priest to inform him exactly and in order about these former citizens. 'You are welcome to hear about them, Solon,' said the priest, 'both for your own sake and for that of the city; and, above all, for the sake of the goddess who is the common patron and protector and educator of both our cities. She founded your city a thousand years before ours, receiving from the Earth and Hephæstus the seed of your race, and then she founded ours, the constitution of which is set down in our sacred registers as 8000 years old. As touching the citizens of 9000 years ago, I will briefly inform you of their laws and of the noblest of their actions; and the exact particulars of the whole we will hereafter go through at our leisure in the sacred registers themselves. If you compare these very laws with your own, you will find that many of ours are the counterpart of yours, as they were in the olden time. In the first place, there is the caste of priests, which is separated from all the others; next there are the artificers, who exercise their several crafts by themselves, and without admixture of any other; and also there is the class of shepherds and that of hunters, as well as that of husbandmen; and you will observe, too, that the warriors in Egypt are separated from all the other classes, and are commanded by the law only to engage in war; moreover, the weapons with which they are equipped are shields and spears, and this the goddess taught first among you, and then in Asiatic countries, and we among the Asiatics first adopted.

"'Then, as to wisdom, do you observe what care the law took from the very first, searching out and comprehending the whole order of things down to prophecy and medicine (the latter with a view to health); and out of these divine elements drawing what was needful for human life, and adding every sort of knowledge which was connected with them. All this order and arrangement the goddess first imparted to you when establishing your city; and she chose the spot of earth in which you were born, because she saw that the happy temperament of the seasons in that land would produce the wisest of men. Wherefore the goddess, who was a lover both of war and of wisdom, selected, and first of all settled that spot which was the most likely to produce men likest herself. And there you dwelt, having such laws as these and still better ones, and excelled all mankind in all virtue, as became the children and disciples of the gods. Many great and wonderful deeds are recorded of your State in our histories; but one of them exceeds all the rest in greatness and valor; for these histories tell of a mighty power which was aggressing wantonly against the whole of Europe and Asia, and to which your city put an end. This power came forth out of the Atlantic Ocean, for in those days the Atlantic was navigable; and there was an island situated in front of the straits which you call the Columns of Heracles: the island was larger than Libya and Asia put together, and was the way to other islands, and from the islands you might pass through the whole of the opposite continent which surrounded the true ocean; for this sea which is within the Straits of Heracles is only a harbor, having a narrow entrance, but that other is a real sea, and the surrounding land may be most truly called a continent. Now, in the island of Atlantis there was a great and wonderful empire, which had rule over the whole island and several others, as well as over parts of the continent; and, besides these, they subjected the parts of Libya within the Columns of Heracles as far as Egypt, and of Europe as far as Tyrrhenia. The vast power thus gathered into one, endeavored to subdue at one blow our country and yours, and the whole of the land which was within the straits; and then, Solon, your country shone forth, in the excellence of her virtue and strength, among all mankind; for she was the first in courage and military skill, and was the leader of the Hellenes. And when the rest fell off from her, being compelled to stand alone, after having undergone the very extremity of danger, she defeated and triumphed over the invaders, and preserved from slavery those who were not yet subjected, and freely liberated all the others who dwelt within the limits of Heracles. But afterward there occurred violent earthquakes and floods, and in a single day and night of rain all your warlike men in a body sunk into the earth, and the island of Atlantis in like manner disappeared, and was sunk beneath the sea. And that is the reason why the sea in those parts is impassable and impenetrable, because there is such a quantity of shallow mud in the way; and this was caused by the subsidence of the island.' ("Plato's Dialogues," ii., 617, *Timæus*.) . . .

"But in addition to the gods whom you have mentioned, I would specially invoke Mnemosyne; for all the important part of what I have to tell is dependent on her favor, and if I can recollect and recite enough of what was said by the priests, and brought hither by Solon, I doubt not that I shall satisfy the requirements of this theatre. To that task, then, I will at once address myself.

"Let me begin by observing, first of all, that nine thousand was the sum of years which had elapsed since the war which was said to have taken place between all those who dwelt outside the Pillars of Heracles and those who dwelt within them: this war I am now to describe. Of the combatants on the one side the city of Athens was reported to have been the ruler, and to have directed the contest; the combatants on the other side were led by the kings of the islands of Atlantis, which, as I was saying, once had an extent greater than that of Libya and Asia; and, when afterward sunk by an earthquake, became an impassable barrier of mud to voyagers sailing from hence to the ocean. The progress of the history will unfold the various tribes of barbarians and Hellenes which then existed, as they successively appear on the scene; but I must begin by describing, first of all, the Athenians as they were in that day, and their enemies who fought with them; and I shall have to tell of the power and form of government of both of them. Let us give the precedence to Athens. . . .

Many great deluges have taken place during the nine thousand years, for that is the number of years which have elapsed since the time of which I am speaking; and in all the ages and changes of things there has never been any settlement of the earth flowing down from the mountains, as in other places, which is worth speaking of; it has always been carried round in a circle, and disappeared in the depths below. The consequence is that, in comparison of what then was, there are remaining in small islets only the bones of the wasted body, as they may be called, all the richer and softer parts of the soil having fallen away, and the mere skeleton of the country being left. . . .

"And next, if I have not forgotten what I heard when I was a child, I will impart to you the character and origin of their adversaries; for friends should not keep their stories to themselves, but have them in common. Yet, before proceeding farther in the narrative, I ought to warn you that you must not be surprised if you should bear Hellenic names given to foreigners. I will tell you the reason of this: Solon, who was intending to use the tale for his poem, made an investigation into the meaning of the names, and found that the early Egyptians, in writing them down, had translated them into their own language, and be recovered the meaning of the several names and retranslated them, and copied them out again in our language. My great-grandfather, Dropidas, had the original writing, which is still in my possession, and was carefully studied by me when I was a child. Therefore, if you bear names such as are used in this country, you must not be surprised, for I have told you the reason of them.

"The tale, which was of great length, began as follows: I have before remarked, in speaking of the allotments of the gods, that they distributed the whole earth into portions differing in extent, and made themselves temples and sacrifices. And Poseidon, receiving for his lot the island of Atlantis, begat children by a mortal woman, and settled them in a part of the island which I will proceed to describe. On the side toward the sea, and in the center of the whole island, there was a plain which is said to have been the fairest of all plains, and very fertile. Near the plain again, and also in the center of the island, at a distance of about fifty stadia, there was a mountain, not very high on any side. In this mountain there dwelt one of the earth-born primeval men of that country, whose name was Evenor, and he had a wife named Leucippe, and they had an only daughter, who was named Cleito. The maiden was growing up to womanhood when her father and mother died; Poseidon fell in love with her, and had intercourse with her; and, breaking the ground, enclosed the hill in which she dwelt all round, making alternate zones of sea and land, larger and smaller, encircling one another; there were two of land and three of water, which he turned as with a lathe out of the center of the island, equidistant every way, so that no man could get to the island, for ships and voyages were not yet heard of. He himself, as he was a god, found no difficulty in making special arrangements for the center island, bringing two streams of water under the earth, which he caused to ascend as springs, one of warm water and the other of cold, and making every variety of food to spring up abundantly in the earth. He also begat and brought up five pairs of male children, dividing the island of Atlantis into ten portions: he gave to the first-born of the eldest pair his mother's dwelling and the surrounding allotment, which was the largest and best, and made him king over the rest; the others he made princes, and gave them rule over many men and a large territory. And he named them all: the eldest, who was king, he named Atlas, and from him the whole island and the ocean received the name of Atlantic. To his twin-brother, who was born after him, and obtained as his lot the extremity of the island toward the Pillars of Heracles, as far as the country which is still called the region of Gades in that part of the world, be gave the name which in the Hellenic language is Eumelus, in the language of the country which is named after him, Gadeirus. Of the second pair of twins, he called one Ampheres and the other Evæmon. To the third pair of twins he gave the name Mneseus to the elder, and

Autochthon to the one who followed him. Of the fourth pair of twins he called the elder Elasippus and the younger Mestor, And of the fifth pair be gave to the elder the name of Azaes, and to the younger Diaprepes. All these and their descendants were the inhabitants and rulers of diverse islands in the open sea; and also, as has been already said, they held sway in the other direction over the country within the Pillars as far as Egypt and Tyrrhenia. Now Atlas had a numerous and honorable family, and his eldest branch always retained the kingdom, which the eldest son handed on to his eldest for many generations; and they had such an amount of wealth as was never before possessed by kings and potentates, and is not likely ever to be again, and they were furnished with everything which they could have, both in city and country. For, because of the greatness of their empire, many things were brought to them from foreign countries, and the island itself provided much of what was required by them for the uses of life. In the first place, they dug out of the earth whatever was to be found there, mineral as well as metal, and that which is now only a name, and was then something more than a name--orichalcum--was dug out of the earth in many parts of the island, and, with the exception of gold, was esteemed the most precious of metals among the men of those days. There was an abundance of wood for carpenters' work, and sufficient maintenance for tame and wild animals. Moreover, there were a great number of elephants in the island, and there was provision for animals of every kind, both for those which live in lakes and marshes and rivers, and also for those which live in mountains and on plains, and therefore for the animal which is the largest and most voracious of them. Also, whatever fragrant things there are in the earth, whether roots, or herbage, or woods, or distilling drops of flowers or fruits, grew and thrived in that land; and again, the cultivated fruit of the earth, both the dry edible fruit and other species of food, which we call by the general name of legumes, and the fruits having a hard rind, affording drinks, and meats, and ointments, and good store of chestnuts and the like, which may be used to play with, and are fruits which spoil with keeping--and the pleasant kinds of dessert which console us after dinner, when we are full and tired of eating--all these that sacred island lying beneath the sun brought forth fair and wondrous in infinite abundance. All these things they received from the earth, and they employed themselves in constructing their temples, and palaces, and harbors, and docks; and they arranged the whole country in the following manner: First of all they bridged over the zones of sea which surrounded the ancient metropolis, and made a passage into and out of they began to build the palace in the royal palace; and then the habitation of the god and of their ancestors. This they continued to ornament in successive generations, every king surpassing the one who came before him to the utmost of his power, until they made the building a marvel to behold for size and for beauty. And, beginning from the sea, they dug a canal three hundred feet in width and one hundred feet in depth, and fifty stadia in length, which they carried through to the outermost zone, making a passage from the sea up to this, which became a harbor, and leaving an opening sufficient to enable the largest vessels to find ingress. Moreover, they divided the zones of land which parted the zones of sea, constructing bridges of such a width as would leave a passage for a single trireme to pass out of one into another, and roofed them over; and there was a way underneath for the ships, for the banks of the zones were raised considerably above the water. Now the largest of the zones into which a passage was cut from the sea was three stadia in breadth, and the zone of land which came next of equal breadth; but the next two, as well the zone of water as of land, were two stadia, and the one which surrounded the central island was a stadium only in width. The island in which the palace was situated had a diameter of five stadia. This, and the zones and the bridge, which was the sixth part of a stadium in width, they surrounded by a stone wall, on either side placing towers, and gates on the bridges where the sea passed in. The stone which was used in the work they quarried from underneath the center island and from underneath the zones, on the outer as well as the inner side. One kind of stone was white, another black, and a third red; and, as they quarried, they at the same time hollowed out docks double within, having roofs formed out of the native rock. Some of their buildings were simple, but in others they put together different stones, which they intermingled for the sake of ornament, to be a natural source of delight. The entire circuit of the wall which went round the outermost one they covered with a coating of brass, and the circuit of the next wall they coated with tin, and the third, which encompassed the citadel flashed with the red light of orichalcum. The palaces in the interior of the citadel were constructed in this wise: In the center was a holy temple dedicated to Cleito and Poseidon, which remained inaccessible, and was surrounded by an enclosure of gold; this was the spot in which they originally begat the race of the ten princes, and thither they annually brought the fruits of the earth in their season from all the ten portions, and performed sacrifices to each of them. Here, too, was Poiseidon's own temple, of a stadium in length and half a stadium in width, and of a proportionate height, having a sort of barbaric splendor. All the outside of the temple, with the exception of the pinnacles, they covered with silver, and the pinnacles with gold. In the interior of the temple the roof was of ivory, adorned everywhere with gold and silver and orichalcum; all the other parts of the walls and pillars and floor they lined with orichalcum. In the temple they placed statues of gold: there was the god himself standing in a chariot--the charioteer of six winged horses--and of such a size that he touched the roof of the building with his head; around him there were a hundred Nereids riding on dolphins, for such was thought to be the number of them in that day. There were also in the interior of the temple other images which had been dedicated by private individuals. And around the temple on the outside were placed statues of gold of all the ten kings and of their wives; and there were many other great offerings, both of kings and of private individuals, coming both from the city itself and the foreign cities over which they held sway. There was an altar, too, which in size and workmanship corresponded to the rest of the work, and there were palaces in like manner which answered to the greatness of the kingdom and the glory of the temple.

"In the next place, they used fountains both of cold and hot springs; these were very abundant, and both kinds wonderfully adapted to use by reason of the sweetness and excellence of their waters. They constructed buildings about them, and planted suitable trees; also cisterns, some open to the heaven, other which they roofed over, to be used in winter as warm baths, there were the king's baths, and the baths of private persons, which were kept apart; also separate baths for women, and others again for horses and cattle, and to them they gave as much adornment as was suitable for them. The water which ran off they carried, some to the grove of Poseidon, where were growing all manner of trees of wonderful height and beauty, owing to the excellence of the soil; the remainder was conveyed by aqueducts which passed over the bridges to the outer circles: and there were many temples built and dedicated to many gods; also gardens and places of exercise, some for men, and some set apart for horses, in both of the two islands formed by the zones; and in the center of the larger of the two there was a race-course of a stadium in width, and in length allowed to extend all round the island, for horses to race in. Also there were guard-houses at intervals for the body-guard, the more trusted of whom had their duties appointed to them in the lesser zone, which was nearer the Acropolis; while the most trusted of all had houses given them within the citadel, and about the persons of the kings. The docks were full of triremes and naval stores, and all things were quite ready for use. Enough of the plan of the royal palace. Crossing the outer harbors, which were three in number, you would come to a wall which began at the sea and went all round: this was everywhere distant fifty stadia from the largest zone and harbor, and enclosed the whole, meeting at the mouth of the channel toward the sea. The entire area was densely crowded with habitations; and the canal and the largest of the harbors were full of vessels and merchants coming from all parts, who, from their numbers, kept up a multitudinous sound of human voices and din of all sorts night and day. I have repeated his descriptions of the city and the parts about the ancient palace nearly as he gave them, and now I must endeavor to describe the nature and arrangement of the rest of the country. The whole country was described as being very lofty and precipitous on the side of the sea, but the country immediately about and surrounding the city was a level plain, itself surrounded by mountains which descended toward the sea; it was smooth and even, but of an oblong shape, extending in one direction three thousand stadia, and going up the country from the sea through the center of the island two thousand stadia; the whole region of the island lies toward the south, and is sheltered from the north. The surrounding mountains he celebrated for their number and size and beauty, in which they exceeded all that are now to be seen anywhere; having in them also many wealthy inhabited villages, and rivers and lakes, and meadows supplying food enough for every animal, wild or tame, and wood of various sorts, abundant for every kind of work. I will now describe the plain, which had been cultivated during many ages by many generations of kings. It was rectangular, and for the most part straight and oblong; and what it wanted of the straight line followed the line of the circular ditch. The depth and width and length of this ditch were incredible and gave the impression that such a work, in addition to so many other works, could hardly have been wrought by the hand of man. But I must say what I have heard. It was excavated to the depth of a hundred feet, and its breadth was a stadium everywhere; it was carried round the whole of the plain, and was ten thousand stadia in length. It received the streams which came down from the mountains, and winding round the plain, and touching the city at various points, was there let off into the sea. From above, likewise, straight canals of a hundred feet in width were cut in the plain, and again let off into the ditch, toward the sea; these canals were at intervals of a Hundred stadia, and by them they brought, down the wood from the mountains to the city, and conveyed the fruits of the earth in ships, cutting transverse passages from one canal into another, and to the city. Twice in the year they gathered the fruits of the earth--in winter having the benefit of the rains, and in summer introducing the water of the canals. As to the population, each of the lots in the plain had an appointed chief of men who were fit for military service, and the size of the lot was to be a square of ten stadia each way, and the total number of all the lots was sixty thousand.

"And of the inhabitants of the mountains and of the rest of the country there was also a vast multitude having leaders, to whom they were assigned according to their dwellings and villages. The leader was required to furnish for the war the sixth portion of a war-chariot, so as to make up a total of ten thousand chariots; also two horses and riders upon them, and a light chariot without a seat, accompanied by a fighting man on foot carrying a small shield, and having a charioteer mounted to guide the horses; also, be was bound to furnish two heavy-armed men, two archers, two slingers, three stone-shooters, and three javelin men, who were skirmishers, and four sailors to make up a complement of twelve hundred ships. Such was the order of war in the royal city--that of the other nine governments was different in each of them, and would be wearisome to narrate. As to offices and honors, the following was the arrangement from the first: Each of the ten kings, in his own division and in his own city, had the absolute control of the citizens, and in many cases of the laws, punishing and slaying whomsoever be would.

"Now the relations of their governments to one another were regulated by the injunctions of Poseidon as the law had handed them down. These were inscribed by the first men on a column of orichalcum, which was situated in the middle of the island, at the temple of Poseidon, whither the people were gathered together every fifth and sixth years alternately, thus giving equal honor to the odd and to the even number. And when they were gathered together they consulted about public affairs, and inquired if anyone had transgressed in anything, and passed judgment on him accordingly--and before they passed judgment they gave their pledges to one another in this wise: There were bulls who had the range of the temple of Poseidon; and the ten who were left alone in the temple, after they had offered prayers to the gods that they might take the sacrifices which were acceptable to them, hunted the bulls without weapons, but with staves and nooses; and the bull which they caught they led up to the column; the victim was then struck on the head by them, and slain over the sacred inscription, Now on the column, besides the law, there was inscribed an oath invoking mighty curses on the disobedient. When, therefore, after offering sacrifice according to their customs, they had burnt the limbs of the bull, they mingled a cup and cast in a clot of blood for each of them; the rest of the victim they took to the fire, after having made a purification of the column all round. Then they drew from the cup in golden vessels, and, pouring a libation on the fire, they swore that they would judge according to the laws on the column, and would punish anyone who had previously transgressed, and that for the future they would not, if they could help, transgress any of the inscriptions, and would not command or obey any ruler who commanded them to act otherwise than according to the laws of their father Poseidon. This was the prayer which each of them offered up for himself and for his family, at the same time drinking, and dedicating the vessel in the temple of the god; and, after spending some necessary time at supper, when darkness came on and the fire about the sacrifice was cool, all of them put on most beautiful azure robes, and, sitting on the ground at night near the embers of the sacrifices on which they had sworn, and extinguishing all the fire about the temple, they received and gave judgement, if any of them had any accusation to bring against any one; and, when they had given judgment, at daybreak they wrote down their sentences on a golden tablet, and deposited them as memorials with their robes. There were many special laws which the several kings had inscribed about the temples, but the most important was the following: That they were not to take up arms against one another, and they were all to come to the rescue if anyone in any city attempted to over. throw the royal house. Like their ancestors, they were to deliberate in common about war and other matters, giving the supremacy to the family of Atlas; and the king was not to have the power of life and death over any of his kinsmen, unless he had the assent of the majority of the ten kings.

"Such was the vast power which the god settled in the lost island of Atlantis; and this he afterward directed against our land on the following pretext, as traditions tell: For many generations, as long as the divine nature lasted in them, they were obedient to the laws, and well-affectioned toward the gods, who were their kinsmen; for they possessed true and in every way great spirits, practicing gentleness and wisdom in the various chances of life, and in their intercourse with one another. They despised everything but virtue, not caring for their present state of life, arid thinking lightly on the possession of gold and other property, which seemed only a burden to them; neither were they intoxicated by luxury; nor did wealth deprive them of their self-control; but they were sober, and saw clearly that all these goods are increased by virtuous friendship with one another, and that by excessive zeal for them, and honor of them, the good of them is lost, and friendship perishes with them.

"By such reflections, and by the continuance in them of a divine nature, all that which we have described waxed and increased in them; but when this divine portion began to fade away in them, and became diluted too often, and with too much of the mortal admixture, and the human nature got the upperhand, then, they being unable to bear their fortune, became unseemly, and to him who had an eye to see, they began to appear base, and had lost the fairest of their precious gifts; but to those who had no eye to see the true happiness, they still appeared glorious and blessed at the very time when they were filled with unrighteous avarice and power. Zeus, the god of gods, who rules with law, and is able to see into such things, perceiving that an honorable race was in a most wretched state, and wanting to inflict punishment on them, that they might be chastened and improved, collected all the gods into his most holy habitation, which, being placed in the center of the world, sees all things that partake of generation. And when he had called them together he spoke as follows:"

[*Here Plato's story abruptly ends.*]

www.ingramcontent.com/pod-product-compliance
Lightning Source LLC
LaVergne TN
LVHW041458070426
835507LV00009B/669